AF228157

AMPHIBIAN GROUPS

BY SUE BRADFORD EDWARDS

An Imprint of Abdo Publishing
abdobooks.com

Cover Image: Many species of tree frogs form groups when it is time for them to mate.

abdobooks.com

Published by Abdo Publishing, a division of ABDO, PO Box 398166, Minneapolis, Minnesota 55439.
Copyright © 2026 by Abdo Consulting Group, Inc. International copyrights reserved in all countries.
No part of this book may be reproduced in any form without written permission from the publisher.
Core Library™ is a trademark and logo of Abdo Publishing.

Printed in the United States of America, North Mankato, Minnesota.
052025
092025

Cover Photo: Abhishek Raviya/Shutterstock Images
Interior Photos: Lisa Pedscalny/Shutterstock Images, 4–5; Shutterstock Images, 6, 9; Jasius/Moment/Getty Images, 11; Christopher Jimenez Nature Photo/Moment Open/Getty Images, 12; Jay Ondreicka/Shutterstock Images, 14–15; Nature and Science/Alamy, 17; McDonald Wildlife Photography Inc./Corbis/Getty Images, 19; David J. Hand/Alamy, 21; Emanuele Biggi/Nature Picture Library/Alamy, 22, 43; Pete Oxford/Danita Delimont/Alamy, 24–25; Red Line Editorial, 27; Natural History Museum, London/Alamy, 30; Jon G. Fuller/VWPics/AP Images, 32–33; Marco Lissoni/Shutterstock Images, 35, 45; Reinhard Dirscherl/Alamy, 36; webguzs/E+/Getty Images, 38; Lucas Bustamante/Nature Picture Library/Alamy, 39; Helmut Göthel Symbiosis/Alamy, 40

Editor: Laura Stickney
Series Designer: Ryan Gale

Library of Congress Control Number: 2024949012

Publisher's Cataloging-in-Publication Data

Names: Edwards, Sue Bradford, author.
Title: Amphibian groups / by Sue Bradford Edwards
Description: Minneapolis, Minnesota: Abdo Publishing, 2026 | Series: Strength in numbers: animal groups | Includes online resources and index.
Identifiers: ISBN 9781098297244 (lib. bdg.) | ISBN 9798384919766 (ebook)
Subjects: LCSH: Amphibians--Juvenile literature. | Amphibian populations--Juvenile literature. | Animal colonies--Juvenile literature. | Amphibians--Behavior--Juvenile literature.
Classification: DDC 597.6--dc23

CONTENTS

NORTHERN RED-LEGGED FROGS

*C*huck-chuck-chuck-chuck-chuck. The northern red-legged frog's chuckling croak is fast and quiet. Several other northern red-legged frogs croak nearby. Around the pond, male frogs hide beneath plants and croak quietly.

Chuck-chuck-chuck-chuck-chuck. It sounds like the frogs are singing together. But they are actually warning each other away. These male frogs have established territories around

Northern red-legged frogs are found along the southwestern coast of Canada and the northwestern coast of the United States. To breed, these frogs require still or slow-moving bodies of water.

FROM EGG TO FROG

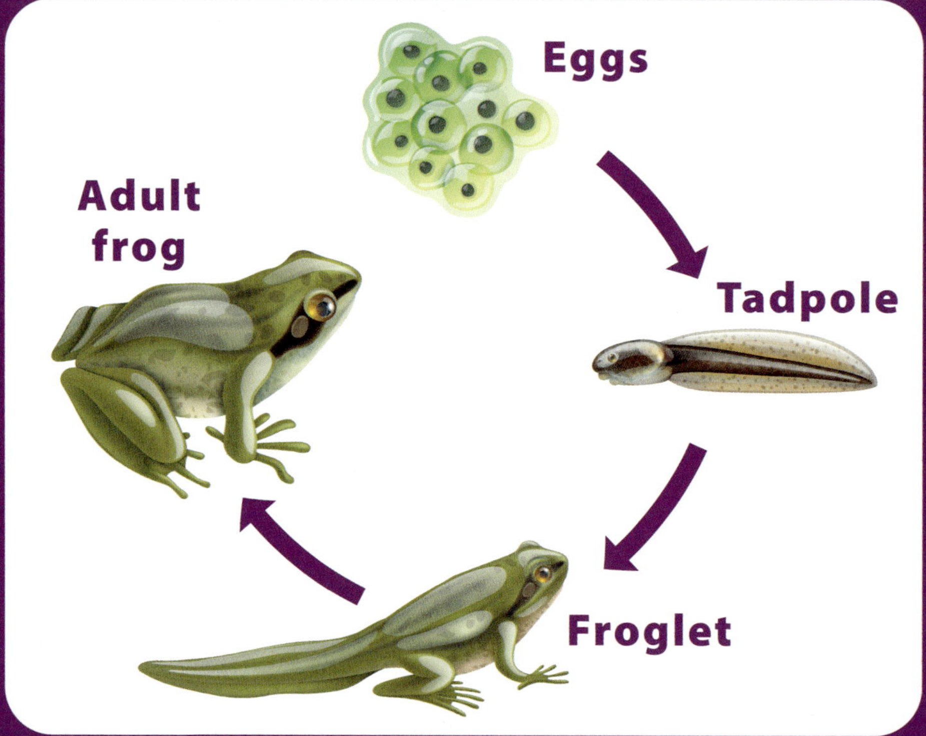

This chart shows the life cycle of a frog. What do you notice about the different stages in the cycle? How do frogs change throughout the cycle?

the pond. Each one is trying to win the attention of a female.

The northern red-legged frog is often reddish brown or gray. It has dark spots. The underside of the frog's lower abdomen and hind legs are red. The frog ranges from about two to five inches (5 to 13 cm) long.

When a female northern red-legged frog is ready to mate, she approaches a croaking male. When the female is close enough, the male wraps his front legs around her. This movement is known as amplexus.

The female lays one egg after another, each one tiny and dark brown. As the female lays the eggs, the male releases a liquid that contains sperm, which fertilizes the eggs. The female may lay as many as 500 to 1,100 eggs, sheltered between water plants such as cattails or bulrushes. The eggs fasten to the plants underwater. They form a mass that is about six to ten inches (15 to 25 cm) across.

AMERICAN TOADS

The American toad can lay anywhere from 4,000 to 20,000 small black eggs. But the female doesn't lay the eggs in a single mass like northern red-legged frogs do. Instead, the toad lays two egg strings that curl and twist around plants in shallow water. The eggs are contained in a clear, jellylike material. The length of the strings varies depending on the number of eggs. They can be 20 to 66 feet (6 to 20 m) long.

It takes 6 to 14 days for the eggs to hatch. When they do, tiny tadpoles emerge. Northern red-legged frogs do not guard their eggs or tadpoles. This means that individual tadpoles make easy meals for predators. To stay safe, newly hatched tadpoles form shoals. A shoal is a group of tadpoles swimming together.

These tadpoles shoal with their brothers and sisters. Predators such as fish are less likely to attack the large group. This means the group of young northern red-legged frogs is more likely to survive. In a few months, the tadpoles that survive grow legs and lungs, becoming froglets. Eventually, the froglets grow into adult frogs.

AMPHIBIANS LIVING TOGETHER

Being part of a group helps animals survive in several ways. Sometimes being in a group provides safety. Predators will often go after group members that are slow, vulnerable, or alone. Because there are so many animals in the group, some group members will survive.

Other times, being in a group helps parents protect their young. Group members can work together to raise young too. Groups also allow animals to share resources that they need to survive.

Amphibians are a group of ectothermic animals. This means they cannot control their body temperature. Instead, they get warmth from their environment. Amphibians include frogs, toads, salamanders, newts, and caecilians.

Frogs and toads are short, four-legged amphibians with mostly moist skin. They move around by hopping or jumping. Groups of frogs are known as armies, colonies, or knots. Frog species include bullfrogs and cane toads.

Newts and salamanders are also amphibians. They look like lizards. They have long, slender bodies and four legs. Unlike lizards, they have no scales. A group of salamanders is called a congress or herd. Salamander species include axolotls and fire-bellied newts.

Caecilians are another type of amphibian. These long, legless animals look like snakes or worms. They burrow in the soil and feed on invertebrates that

CANE TOADS

Northern red-legged frog tadpoles aren't the only ones that swim in groups. Cane toad tadpoles have been found swimming at the bottoms of ponds in groups called schools. These schools may contain tens of thousands of tadpoles. When a tadpole is scared or hurt by a predator, it gives off a chemical called a pheromone. When other tadpoles in the school are exposed to this chemical, they mature into frogs more quickly. This allows them to leave an area that has a lot of predators.

Alpine newts form groups during the breeding season.
They also gather to hibernate during the winter.

live there. Some caecilian species include the Eastern

Peru caecilian and the pointed-headed caecilian.

Amphibians form groups for specific reasons.

Some, such as strawberry poison frogs, come together

to mate and reproduce. Other amphibians find safety

in numbers when they lay their eggs. Parent-offspring

groups form as amphibians raise and protect their

young. These animals may also form groups when

looking for shelter from cold or dry weather.

STRAIGHT TO THE
SOURCE

Froglife is a reptile and amphibian conservation organization. An article on its website talks about how tadpoles form groups with family members:

> *Swimming around in the open water, tadpoles are highly vulnerable to [predators] so in many species . . . tadpoles swim in large groups or shoals. By living in groups the tadpoles gain advantages such as decreased risks of [predators] and increased access to food. . . . Tadpoles further increase the benefits of group living by associating with relatives, or close kin. If forming shoals reduces the risk of [predators], then swimming with relatives who possess similar genes will increase the chances that these genes will survive to the next generation.*

> Source: "Croaking Science: Kin Recognition." *Froglife*, 31 May 2018, froglife.org. Accessed 6 Nov. 2024.

CONSIDER YOUR AUDIENCE

Adapt this passage for a different audience, such as your friends. Write a blog post conveying this same information for the new audience. How does your post differ from the original text and why?

SALAMANDERS

Hellbenders are the largest salamanders in the United States. Adults range in size from 12 to 29 inches (30 to 74 cm) long and can weigh up to five pounds (2 kg). Their color varies from muddy brown to gray or black, and they have wide, flat heads with tiny eyes. These amphibians have adapted to live in fast-flowing streams. Hellbenders live in the central and eastern United States, from Missouri in the west to New York in the east. They can also

A hellbender's brownish coloring and flat body help it blend into the surroundings of its rocky habitat. The salamander's wrinkled skin helps it take in oxygen.

be found as far south as northern Mississippi, Alabama, and Georgia.

Hellbenders are ambush hunters, which means they sit at the bottom of streams and wait for prey to swim nearby. When a crayfish or small fish passes by, the hellbender grabs it. The salamander's color helps camouflage it from prey. But hellbenders also hide beneath large rocks with only their heads poking out.

Hellbenders usually live alone until it's time to mate. During mating time, ten or more hellbenders gather in one area. A male hellbender digs a burrow under a large rock and waits for a female to enter the burrow.

During breeding season, male hellbenders often fight other males to gain control of nesting sites or defend their burrows.

Once inside, the female lays two strings of up to 400 eggs in a yellowish, softball-size mass. The male fertilizes the eggs as the female lays them. When the female is done, the male chases her out of the burrow and then stands guard over the eggs.

The male protects the eggs from predators, including other hellbenders. He also rocks back and forth over the eggs. This motion stirs the water, bringing oxygen to the eggs.

The male guards the eggs for 68 to 75 days until they hatch. Hatchlings are about 1 to 1.25 inches (2.5 to 3.2 cm) long. They breathe through gills. A group of hellbenders is more likely to survive until this stage because the male guards the unhatched eggs. Predators will try to eat the hatchlings, but at this point, the male hellbender's job is done.

FOUR-TOED SALAMANDER

Like hellbenders, four-toed salamanders also guard their eggs. These amphibians range from two to four inches (5 to 10 cm) long. They are rusty brown or grayish brown in color. They eat insects such as beetles, flies, and ants. Sometimes they eat spiders and snails too.

The four-toed salamander has a large range. It can be found from Nova Scotia, Canada, to the Gulf of Mexico. However, four-toed salamanders do not live throughout this entire area because they live only

where they can find specific resources. Although the salamanders nest on land and find food in forests, they need wetland areas for breeding.

When it is time to mate, a male four-toed salamander rubs his nose on a female's nose. If the female accepts him, she presses her nose to the base of his tail, and the male drops spermatophores. These globs contain sperm. The female picks these spermatophores up and inserts them into her cloaca. The eggs are then fertilized inside the female's body. When she is ready to lay the eggs, the female moves to a nesting site.

Female salamanders make or find a hollow in which they can lay their eggs. They must find a nesting site that is located just above the water in a swampy area or pond. The salamander looks for moss, leaf litter, rotting logs, or clumps of grass.

Each egg takes the female several minutes to lay, and it may take hours to lay the full clutch of eggs. A clutch can contain between 15 and 80 eggs. Larger females often lay more eggs than smaller ones do.

Scientists have found as many as

ARBOREAL SALAMANDERS

Arboreal salamanders have no lungs. They breathe through their skin, which they must keep damp. When it is too dry outside, the salamanders seek shelter in places such as tree cavities. Scientists have found groups containing a dozen arboreal salamanders or more. Because they are ectothermic, these amphibians do not share body heat. But grouping together allows them to share the limited sheltered spaces that help them survive.

Many types of salamanders, such as marbled salamanders, lay their eggs in leaf litter. This provides moisture and shelter.

Many salamander species guard their eggs. Female Strinati's cave salamanders often guard their eggs for as long as ten months, coiling their bodies around the eggs.

1,110 four-toed salamander eggs in a single nest.

Because of this, they know that females share nests.

Females may do this to help each other protect the

eggs. But they may also do it simply because there are a

limited number of good nesting sites. Usually, only one female stays with the nest until the eggs hatch, which takes about 38 to 62 days.

Females are not usually aggressive toward predators, but their presence in the nest keeps predators away. Having a female guard the nesting site means more eggs will survive long enough to hatch. Some scientists also think that a female's skin oozes a substance that keeps fungi from growing on the eggs. This guarded group nest helps a greater number of four-toed salamander eggs survive.

EXPLORE ONLINE

Chapter Two discusses the hellbender. The article at the website below goes into more depth on this topic. Does the article answer any questions you had about hellbenders?

HELLBENDER

abdocorelibrary.com/amphibian-groups

CAECILIANS

Scientists do not know much about the more than 200 species of caecilians living around the globe. This is partially because most caecilian species live their entire lives in underground burrows. These mysterious amphibians push their way headfirst through the soil. They live mainly in the tropics, an area of Earth along the equator that tends to be hot, sunny, and wet.

One thing scientists do know about caecilians is that some species form groups to

Many types of caecilians, including ringed caecilians, have wormlike bodies, moist skin, and small eyes.

SURINAM TOADS

When Surinam toads mate, the male spreads the eggs across the female's back. It takes up to one day for the eggs to sink into the female's skin. The skin covers the eggs, forming a pocket around each one. The eggs develop there. After hatching, the tadpoles remain under the skin until they grow into toadlets. Only then do the young toads detach from the mother's back, temporarily leaving round holes behind in her skin.

care for their young. One species is the *Boulengerula taitana*, also known as the Taita African caecilian, the Taita Hills caecilian, or the Taita Mountains caecilian. It lives in Kenya.

Taita African caecilians usually mate at the start of the rainy season, which lasts from October to December. After they mate, female Taita African caecilians build underground nests that are approximately 1.6 by 1.4 by 1.3 inches (4 by 3.6 by 3.3 cm) big. These nests are hidden about 2 to 28 inches (5 to 71 cm) beneath the ground. Many times, nests are clustered together, and adult Taita African caecilians live among the nests. Some live near their

WHERE CAECILIANS
LIVE

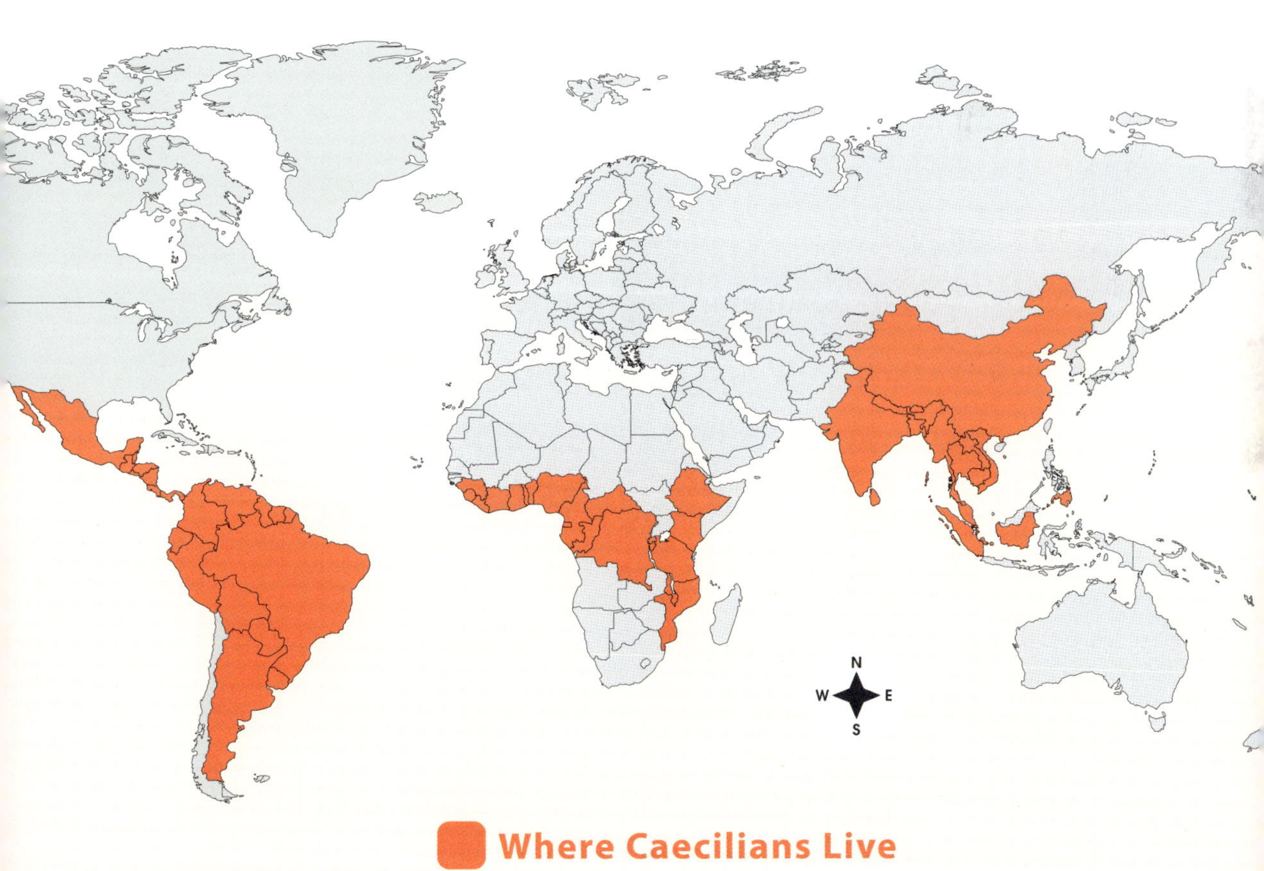

Where Caecilians Live

own nests, while others may have no eggs of their own in the surrounding nests. Having nests close together allows the caecilians to care for the group's offspring, rather than just their own.

In her nest, a female Taita African caecilian lays between one and ten eggs. When the eggs hatch, the female grows a heavy skin. Layers of this heavy skin are peeled off and eaten by the young animals.

RINGED CAECILIANS

The Taita African caecilian isn't the only caecilian whose young eat from their mother's skin. Another is *Siphonops annulatus,* or the ringed caecilian. It is blue-gray in color and lives in South America. Adult ringed caecilians eat worms, crickets, snails, slugs, and termites.

Female ringed caecilians make space for their eggs on the surface of the forest floor in shallow nests. These nests are cradled among tree roots, which form the nest walls. Each female lays a clutch of 5 to 16 eggs and curls her body around the eggs in the nest. Scientists have never seen a female ringed caecilian act aggressively toward a predator, but the female's presence in the nest protects the eggs from snakes, ants, and burrowing mammals.

By the time the eggs hatch, the mother has grown a special skin that has extra lipids, or fats. These fats provide nutrition for the young ringed caecilians. Because the young have special teeth, they can tear this skin off and eat it. It takes the mother at least 64 hours to regrow these special skin cells between feedings.

HORNED MARSUPIAL FROGS

Like ringed caecilians, horned marsupial frogs guard their eggs. But female frogs do so by carrying the eggs around. When these South American frogs mate, the male puts the fertilized eggs in a pouch on the female's back. The female carries the eggs around for 60 to 80 days as they develop. The eggs hatch into fully developed froglets, skipping the tadpole stage. Then the female opens the pouch and lets the froglets out.

Ringed caecilian hatchlings make clicking noises to let their mother know when they're hungry. When the mother hears these clicks, she produces milky liquid for her young to eat.

Because of this delay, the ringed caecilian has a second way to nourish its young. In the nest, the mother coils her body and raises her hind end. A special liquid oozes from her cloaca. This nutritious liquid is made of amino acids, sugars, fats, and cells from the ducts that carry eggs from within the mother's body.

The mother produces this milky liquid for approximately two months. By the time she is done feeding her young, the female ringed caecilian has changed from blue-gray to white. Because the mothers do not leave the nest to hunt while caring for their young, they lose as much as 30 percent of their body weight. Although feeding the young is difficult work, these mother-offspring groups ensure that more young ringed caecilians reach adulthood.

FURTHER EVIDENCE

Chapter Three of this book discusses how Taita African caecilians and ringed caecilians feed and care for their young. What was one of the main points of this chapter? What evidence is included to support this point? Read the article at the website below. Does the information on the website support the main point of the chapter? Does it present new evidence?

CAECILIAN

abdocorelibrary.com/amphibian-groups

POISON DART FROGS

Poison dart frogs are known for their bright colors and are commonly found in tropical regions. Their colors are a warning. These tiny frogs contain poison in their skin, making them toxic to predators. Strawberry poison frogs are red with tiny dark spots and blue legs. They range in size from less than an inch to 2.5 inches (6.4 cm). They live in the rainforests of Central America and South America. Some strawberry poison frogs can be found in Hawaii.

Strawberry poison frogs are sometimes called blue jeans poison dart frogs. These tiny amphibians can climb plants and leaves high above the forest floor.

DARWIN FROGS

A male Darwin frog guards his fertilized eggs from predators. But that's not all this South American frog does. A few days before the eggs hatch, the male gulps them down and stores them in his vocal sac. This sac is what enables frogs to croak. In the safety of the male frog's vocal sac, the eggs hatch and the tadpoles grow. They feed on a substance that oozes from a gland in the male's vocal sac. Then the male releases the tiny frogs.

A male strawberry poison frog has his own territory. This may be a small area with many females nearby. Female frogs look for good places to raise tadpoles. The frogs mate when it is wet or damp outside. The male calls out, and the female frog follows the sound of his call. The male and female frogs sit facing away from each other. The female lays about six pea-size eggs in wet leaf litter on the forest floor. Then the male releases sperm to fertilize the eggs.

The male frog guards the eggs, preventing other male strawberry poison frogs from eating them.

He removes any fungi that have grown on the eggs. He also waters them by peeing on them. The male rotates the eggs too. If he has mated with several females, the male frog must take care of several clutches. In 10 to 12 days, the tadpoles hatch.

Once the tadpoles hatch, their mother cares for them. She sits so that a tadpole can swim onto her back. Then she carries it up into a tree, where the tadpole drops into a water-filled plant called a bromeliad.

The female frog carries each tadpole to its own pool of water. She puts each tadpole in its own pool so larger tadpoles cannot eat the smaller ones.

After this, the female strawberry poison frog still has work to do. Every day, she climbs up to each tadpole to feed it. She does this by lowering herself into the water and laying between one and five unfertilized eggs. She does this every day. It takes 43 to 52 days for the tadpoles to mature into frogs.

BLUE POISON DART FROGS

Another poison dart frog that cares for its young is the blue poison dart frog. These bright-blue frogs are flecked with black spots and live in the South American country of Suriname. The females lay five to ten eggs, which the male cares for much like a male strawberry poison frog does. When a tadpole hatches, it holds onto the male's back with its mouth. The male carries it to a pool in a tree branch or flower. There, the female takes over the tadpole's care, feeding it unfertilized eggs.

In 2019, scientists studied several poison dart frog species in

MOUNTAIN YELLOW-LEGGED FROGS

Many frogs overwinter at the bottom of lakes and ponds. Mountain yellow-legged frogs have been found overwintering in groups of eight or more. They gather where water is heavily oxygenated and deep enough not to freeze. These are the two things frogs need to survive the winter. Sharing these spaces in small groups helps larger numbers of frogs survive the cold months.

South America. They studied three-striped poison dart frogs in Peru and dyeing poison dart frogs in French Guiana. The frogs showed a pattern of childcare. In both species, the male guards the eggs until they hatch and then carries the tadpoles to a pool of water, such as a pond or flooded pasture. The three-striped poison dart frog males carried their tadpoles the farthest, traveling an average of 705 feet (215 m) and passing other pools along the way. Scientists do not know why the male frogs pass some pools. The poison dart frogs also use

Three-striped poison dart frogs are known for their green-and-black coloring. Males sometimes carry several tadpoles at a time.

parent-offspring groups to make sure their eggs survive long enough to hatch into tadpoles.

Being part of a group is one of the adaptations that enables amphibians to survive. Sometimes these groups share resources, such as food or nesting sites. Groups also make it easier for adult frogs to guard eggs so the young have time to mature and hatch. Other groups keep their young nearby so adults can feed them. Groups help amphibians survive and thrive in many habitats around the world.

STRAIGHT TO THE
SOURCE

Dr. Isabella Capellini works at Queen's University Belfast. In 2021, she studied how amphibian species care for their young. She said:

> *Our work in this study demonstrates that species such as some Malagasy poison frogs . . . have larger eggs in smaller clutches, but different forms of parental care have different influence on the trade off between egg size and egg number. For example, species that brood their eggs or tadpoles on or inside the body can only care for few large eggs, likely because the parent's body has limited room. However, those that guard their eggs can afford to protect larger eggs without reducing clutch size. Instead, frogs that feed their [young] have few small eggs, probably because constant feeding after hatching makes producing initially large eggs unnecessary.*

> Source: "Researchers Discover How Amphibians Differ in Caring for Their Young." *Queen's University Belfast*, 7 Jan. 2022, qub.ac.uk. Accessed 6 Nov. 2024.

BACK IT UP

The author of this passage is using evidence to support a point. Write a paragraph describing the point the author is making. Then write down two or three pieces of evidence the author uses to make the point.

FAST FACTS

- Amphibians are a group of ectothermic animals. They get warmth from their environment instead of producing their own body heat. Amphibians include frogs, toads, salamanders, newts, and caecilians.

- Northern red-legged frog tadpoles swim in large groups called shoals. This can protect them from predators.

- The tadpoles of some frog species swim in groups that number in the thousands.

- In parent-offspring groups, amphibians care for their young. Male hellbenders guard their eggs until they hatch.

- Female four-toed salamanders care for their eggs. Multiple females lay eggs in the same nest. Then one female stands guard until the eggs hatch, ensuring that more eggs survive.

- In some parent-offspring groups, amphibians feed their young. Young Taita African caecilians feed on strips of their mother's loose skin.

- Female ringed caecilians produce a milky liquid to feed their young.

- Poison dart frogs form parent-offspring groups. The male frogs often guard the eggs. When the eggs hatch, the frogs carry the tadpoles to pools of water. Some female poison dart frogs lay unfertilized eggs for the young to eat.

Tell the Tale

Chapter Three of this book discusses caecilians that live in tropical regions. Imagine you are exploring the tropics looking for caecilians to study. Write 200 words about the caecilians you encounter on your trip. What do you notice about these amphibians?

Take a Stand

This book talks about the natural habitats that amphibians need to survive. Do you think people should do more to protect these habitats? If so, what do you think should be done to protect them? Why?

Why Do I Care?

Maybe you do not live near a place with many amphibians. But that doesn't mean you can't think about why these animals are important. What can you learn by studying amphibians? What do these animals teach you about group behavior?

You Are There

This book discusses poison dart frogs in the rainforest.
Imagine you are traveling through the rainforest with
scientists who study poison dart frogs. Write a letter home
telling your friends what you see during your travels. What
do you notice about the frogs and their habitats? Be sure to
add plenty of detail to your notes.

GLOSSARY

adapt
to change or develop in order to be better suited to an environment

amino acids
the building blocks that make up proteins

cloaca
an opening on an animal's body through which waste such as urine, feces, sperm, or eggs leave the body

fertilize
to join male and female cells to produce young

invertebrate
an animal that does not have a backbone

mature
to develop or grow

overwinter
to wait out or pass through the winter

oxygenate
to combine or mix with oxygen

territory
an area of land that animals live in and defend from others

toxic
poisonous or harmful

vulnerable
in danger of being attacked or harmed

ONLINE RESOURCES

To learn more about amphibian groups, visit our free resource websites below.

Visit **abdocorelibrary.com** or scan this QR code for free Common Core resources for teachers and students, including vetted activities, multimedia, and booklinks, for deeper subject comprehension.

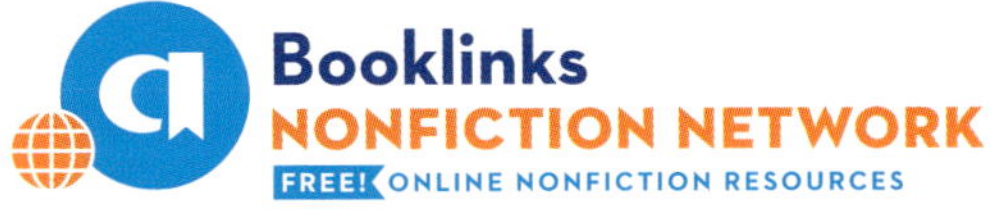

Visit **abdobooklinks.com** or scan this QR code for free additional online weblinks for further learning. These links are routinely monitored and updated to provide the most current information available.

LEARN MORE

Fickett, Jamie. *Crazy Frogs*. Seahorse, 2025.

Howard, Jules. *Encyclopedia of Animals*. Chartwell, 2022.

Seigel, Rachel. *Amphibians*. Abdo, 2023.

INDEX

About the Author

Sue Bradford Edwards grew up in Missouri watching every PBS special on animals that she could find. She is now a Missouri nonfiction author who writes about science, social sciences, and culture. She has written more than 60 books for young readers, including several books about animals.